Spring into Mental Maths with CGP!

The daffodils are out, lambs are in the fields, the days are getting longer... it must be time for some Mental Maths Daily Practice from CGP!

This brilliant book covers a huge range of skills from the Year 5 curriculum, with a page of practice for every day of the spring term.

And it doesn't stop there — this treasure trove of examples and colourful pictures will keep pupils engaged in class and at home. Spring-tastic!

What CGP is all about

Our sole aim here at CGP is to produce the highest quality books — carefully written, immaculately presented and dangerously close to being funny.

Then we work our socks off to get them out to you — at the cheapest possible prices.

Contents

☑ Use the tick boxes to help keep a record of which tests have been attempted.

Week 1
- ☑ Day 1 1
- ☑ Day 2 2
- ☑ Day 3 3
- ☑ Day 4 4
- ☑ Day 5 5

Week 2
- ☑ Day 1 6
- ☑ Day 2 7
- ☑ Day 3 8
- ☑ Day 4 9
- ☑ Day 5 10

Week 3
- ☑ Day 1 11
- ☑ Day 2 12
- ☑ Day 3 13
- ☑ Day 4 14
- ☑ Day 5 15

Week 4
- ☑ Day 1 16
- ☑ Day 2 17
- ☑ Day 3 18
- ☑ Day 4 19
- ☑ Day 5 20

Week 5
- ☑ Day 1 21
- ☑ Day 2 22
- ☑ Day 3 23
- ☑ Day 4 24
- ☑ Day 5 25

Week 6
- ☑ Day 1 26
- ☑ Day 2 27
- ☑ Day 3 28
- ☑ Day 4 29
- ☑ Day 5 30

Week 7
- ☑ Day 1 31
- ☑ Day 2 32
- ☑ Day 3 33
- ☑ Day 4 34
- ☑ Day 5 35

Week 8
- ☑ Day 1 36
- ☑ Day 2 37
- ☑ Day 3 38
- ☑ Day 4 39
- ☑ Day 5 40

Week 9

- [✓] Day 1 41
- [✓] Day 2 42
- [✓] Day 3 43
- [✓] Day 4 44
- [✓] Day 5 45

Week 10

- [✓] Day 1 46
- [✓] Day 2 47
- [✓] Day 3 48
- [✓] Day 4 49
- [✓] Day 5 50

Week 11

- [✓] Day 1 51
- [✓] Day 2 52
- [✓] Day 3 53
- [✓] Day 4 54
- [✓] Day 5 55

Week 12

- [✓] Day 1 56
- [✓] Day 2 57
- [✓] Day 3 58
- [✓] Day 4 59
- [✓] Day 5 60

Answers 61

Published by CGP

ISBN: 978 1 78908 771 0

Editors: Ellen Burton, Katie Fernandez, Claire Plowman and Tamara Sinivassen
With thanks to Emma Clayton and Tina Ramsden for the proofreading.
With thanks to Lottie Edwards for the copyright research.

Clipart from Corel®

Printed by Elanders Ltd, Newcastle upon Tyne.
Based on the classic CGP style created by Richard Parsons.

Text, design, layout and original illustrations © Coordination Group Publications Ltd. (CGP) 2021
All rights reserved.

Photocopying this book is not permitted, even if you have a CLA licence.
Extra copies are available from CGP with next day delivery • 0800 1712 712 • www.cgpbooks.co.uk

How to Use this Book

- This book contains 60 daily practice tests.
- We've split them into 12 sections — that's roughly one for each week of the Year 5 spring term.
- Each week is made up of 5 tests, so there's one for every school day of the term (Monday – Friday).
- Each test should take about 5-10 minutes to complete.
- Pupils should aim to do their working in their heads, without writing anything down.
- The tests contain a mix of topics from Year 5 Mental Maths. New Year 5 topics are gradually introduced as you go through the book.
- The tests increase in difficulty as you progress through the term.
- Each test looks something like this:

The Week and the Day of the test are shown at the top of the page.

The instruction the pupil needs to follow is in the box at the top of the page.

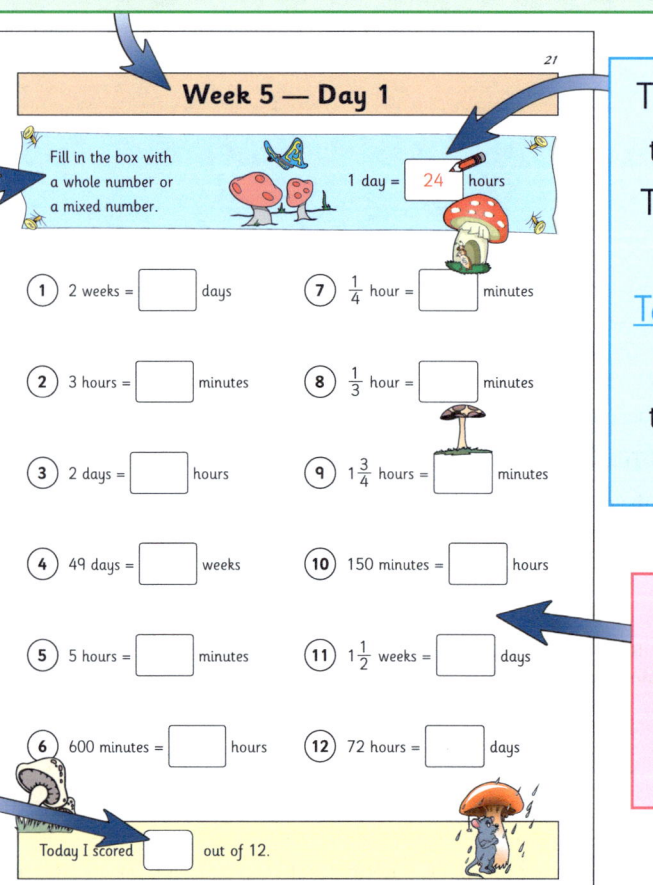

There's an example at the top of the page. The correct answer is shown in red. Talk the pupil through the instruction and the example so they know what to do.

There are between 4 and 14 questions for the pupil to answer.

There's a score box at the bottom of the test. Use this to keep track of how well the pupil has done.

Week 1 — Day 1

Fill in the missing number.

$0.27 = \dfrac{27}{100}$

1) $0.3 = \dfrac{\Box}{10}$

2) $0.7 = \dfrac{\Box}{10}$

3) $0.5 = \dfrac{\Box}{2}$

4) $0.39 = \dfrac{\Box}{100}$

5) $0.83 = \dfrac{\Box}{100}$

6) $0.91 = \dfrac{\Box}{100}$

7) $0.25 = \dfrac{\Box}{4}$

8) $0.75 = \dfrac{\Box}{4}$

9) $0.2 = \dfrac{\Box}{5}$

10) $0.8 = \dfrac{\Box}{5}$

11) $0.4 = \dfrac{\Box}{20}$

12) $0.9 = \dfrac{\Box}{20}$

Today I scored ☐ out of 12.

Week 1 — Day 2

Chloe drew a bar chart showing the number of new flowers in her garden each day. Between which two days was the difference from one day to the following day the greatest? What was the difference?

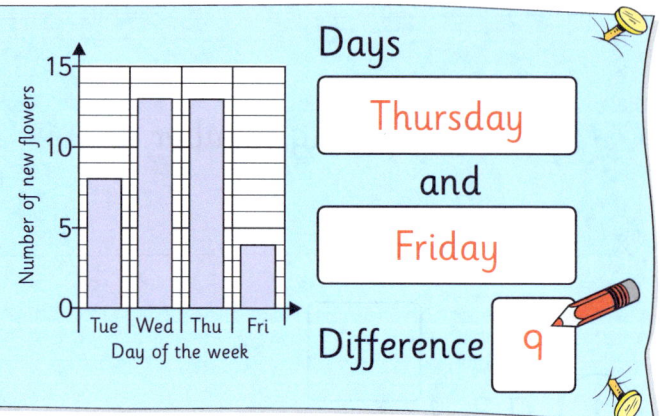

Days: **Thursday** and **Friday**
Difference: **9**

1) Days _____ and _____ Difference ____

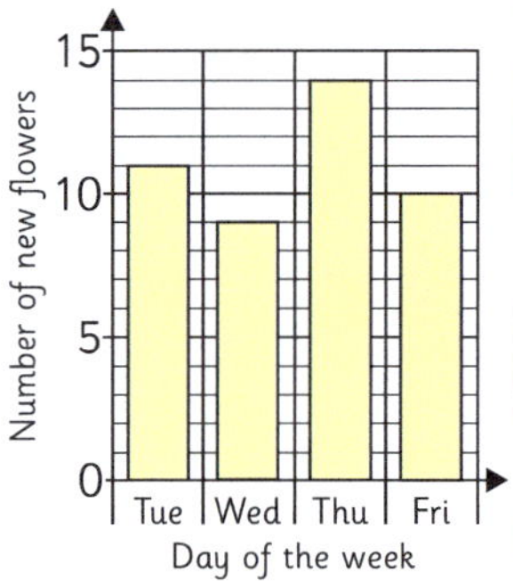

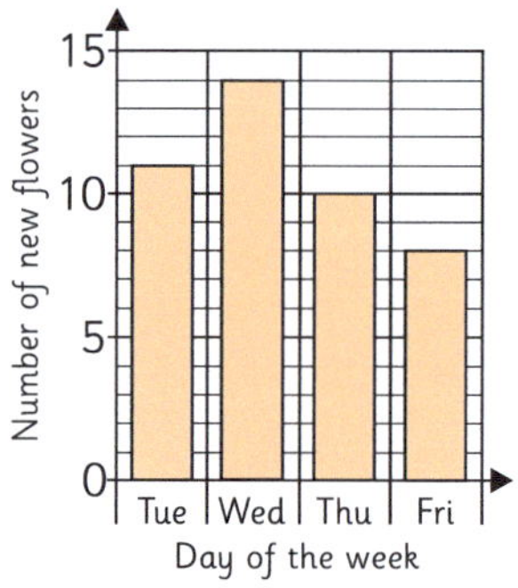

2) 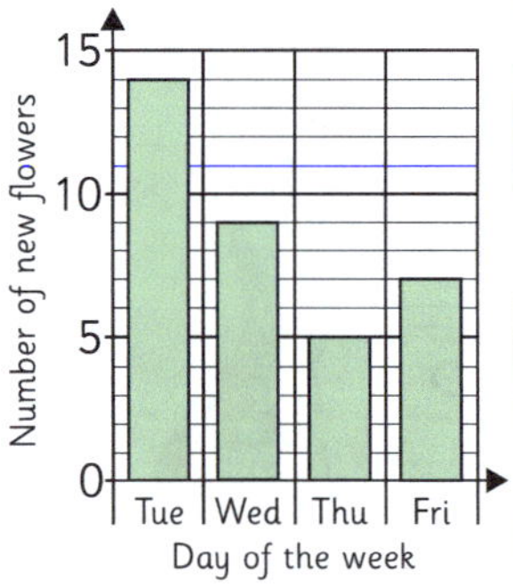 Days _____ and _____ Difference ____

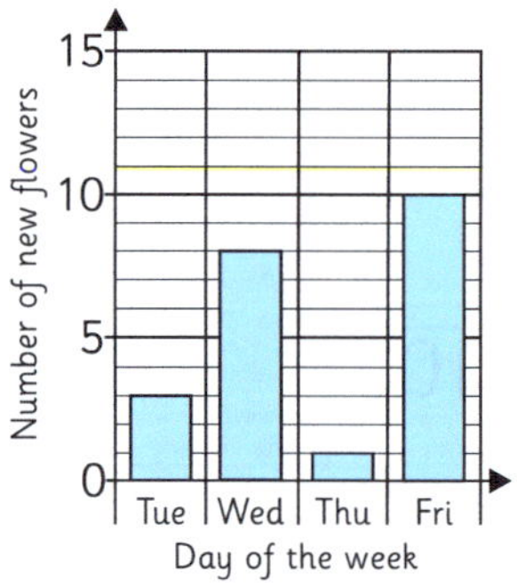

3) Days _____ and _____ Difference ____

4) Days _____ and _____ Difference ____

5) Days _____ and _____ Difference ____

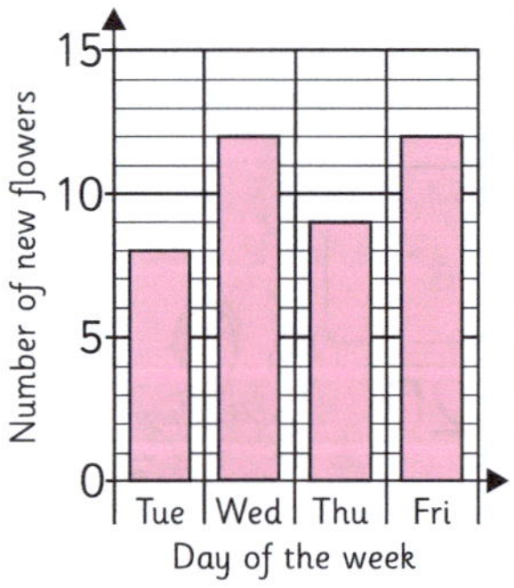

6) Days _____ and _____ Difference ____

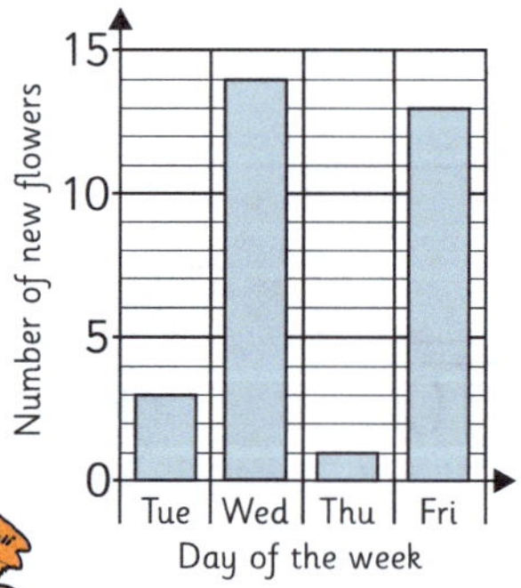

Today I scored ____ out of 6.

Year 5 Mental Maths — Spring Term

Week 1 — Day 3

Fill in the missing number.
Use the number line to help you.

$-6 - 2 = \boxed{-8}$

$\leftarrow$ –10 –9 –8 –7 –6 –5 –4 –3 –2 –1 0 1 2 3 4 5 6 7 8 9 10 $\rightarrow$

1) $-4 + 3 = \boxed{}$

2) $-7 + \boxed{} = -3$

3) $-2 - 7 = \boxed{}$

4) $-3 + \boxed{} = 7$

5) $-9 + 12 = \boxed{}$

6) $-6 + \boxed{} = 9$

7) $8 - 13 = \boxed{}$

8) $\boxed{} - 5 = -8$

9) $\boxed{} - 8 = -2$

10) $\boxed{} - 11 = -8$

11) $-4 - \boxed{} = -9$

12) $\boxed{} + 5 = -2$

Today I scored $\boxed{}$ out of 12.

Week 1 — Day 4

Fill in the operation for the sequence and any missing numbers.

Operation: **− 1000**

27 438 — 26 438 — **25 438** →

1) Operation: ☐

82 324 — 82 334 — ☐ — 82 354 — ☐ →

2) Operation: ☐

56 501 — 56 701 — ☐ — 57 101 — ☐ →

3) Operation: ☐

6893 — 6863 — ☐ — 6803 — ☐ →

4) Operation: ☐

529 — 2529 — ☐ — 6529 — ☐ →

5) Operation: ☐

43 318 — 38 318 — ☐ — 28 318 — ☐ →

6) Operation: ☐

70 078 — 55 078 — ☐ — 25 078 — ☐ →

Today I scored ☐ out of 6.

Year 5 Mental Maths — Spring Term

Week 1 — Day 5

If the children share their marbles equally between them, how many marbles will each child get?

Alf has 8, Bella has 9 and Cai has 4.

7

1. Dot has 6, Ed has 4 and Flo has 5.

2. Guy has 4, Haf has 7, Ian has 8, Jo has 6 and Kev has 5.

3. Lia has 12, Mo has 8, Noa has 9 and Obi has 3.

4. Peg has 11, Quinn has 13, Raj has 6 and Sal has 10.

5. Tom has 3, Uma has 21 and Vic has 12.

6. Wen has 8, Xue has 9, Yi has 20, Zac has 5 and Ada has 8.

7. Bai has 22, Cat has 36 and Dom has 2.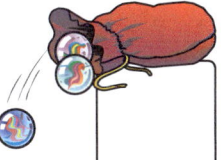

8. Ece has 13, Fin has 13 and Gia has 19.

9. Hui has 19, Ivy has 21, Jai has 17 and Kim has 23.

10. Lou has 18, Mae has 6 and Ned has 6.

11. Ona has 4, Pip has 12, Ros has 7 and Sid has 9.

12. Tia has 15, Udi has 15, Vi has 12, Will has 10, Xia has 9 and Yun has 11.

Today I scored ☐ out of 12.

Week 2 — Day 1

Solve the calculation. 13.1 × 100 = 1310

1) 851 × 10 =

2) 25 ÷ 10 =

3) 3.24 × 100 =

4) 7553 ÷ 100 =

5) 44.12 × 10 =

6) 350 ÷ 100 =

7) 1.2 × 1000 =

8) 7 ÷ 100 =

9) 55.66 × 100 =

10) 6080 ÷ 1000 =

11) 0.33 × 1000 =

12) 1850 ÷ 1000 =

Today I scored ☐ out of 12.

Week 2 — Day 2

Write the answer in the box.

Alice had £30 in her piggy bank. She spent £3, then was given £5. How much does she have now?   £32

1) Ola had £25 in her piggy bank. She spent £2, then was given £3.50. How much does she have now?

2) Kyle had £35 in his piggy bank. He spent £6, then won £2.10. How much does he have now?

3) Minnie had £24 in her piggy bank. She spent £12, then was given £6.75. How much does she have now?

4) Fardeen had £21.50 in his piggy bank. He spent £2, then earned £9. How much does he have now?

5) Rachael had £36.60 in her piggy bank. She spent £3.40, then won £15. How much does she have now?

6) Theodore had £22.30 in his piggy bank. He spent £2.95, then was given 50p. How much does he have now?

7) Jasmine had £32.50 in her piggy bank. She spent £3.20, then received £2.05. How much does she have now?

8) Elis had £18.60 in his piggy bank. He spent £6.70, then was given 90p. How much does he have now?

Today I scored ☐ out of 8.

Week 2 — Day 3

Circle the best estimate for the measurement. The mass of a banana.

1.3 g | (130 g) | 1.3 kg | 13 kg

1. The height of an adult person.
   1.7 cm | 17 cm | 1.7 m | 17 m

2. The mass of a football.
   0.42 g | 4.2 g | 420 g | 42 kg

3. The length of a skipping rope.
   2.7 mm | 27 mm | 27 cm | 2.7 m

4. The capacity of a mug.
   350 ml | 3.5 l | 35 l | 350 l

5. The length of a pencil.
   10 mm | 10 cm | 1 m | 10 m

6. The mass of a loaf of bread.
   4 g | 400 g | 4 kg | 40 kg

7. The height of a daffodil.
   40 mm | 40 cm | 4 m | 40 m

8. The capacity of a milk bottle.
   0.57 ml | 5.7 ml | 570 ml | 57 l

9. The width of a netball court.
   15.3 cm | 153 cm | 15.3 m | 153 m

10. The length of a bus.
    13 mm | 13 cm | 13 m | 13 km

11. The mass of a hamster.
    0.3 g | 30 g | 3 kg | 30 kg

12. The capacity of a can of soup.
    0.4 ml | 4 ml | 40 ml | 400 ml

Today I scored ☐ out of 12.

Week 2 — Day 4

Circle all common factors of the numbers in the yellow boxes.

15
27

(1), 2, (3), 5, 6, 8, 9

1. 8 / 12 — 1, 2, 3, 5, 6, 8, 9
2. 16 / 24 — 2, 3, 4, 6, 7, 8, 9
3. 10 / 25 — 1, 2, 5, 6, 8, 9, 10
4. 11 / 44 — 2, 3, 5, 6, 7, 9, 11
5. 21 / 35 — 2, 3, 5, 6, 7, 9, 11
6. 16 / 44 — 2, 3, 4, 5, 6, 8, 9
7. 40 / 90 — 1, 3, 4, 5, 8, 9, 10
8. 36 / 45 — 4, 5, 6, 9, 12, 15
9. 15 / 60 — 2, 3, 5, 6, 10, 15
10. 24 / 56 — 2, 3, 5, 6, 7, 8, 12
11. 18 / 45 — 1, 3, 5, 6, 8, 9, 15
12. 48 / 72 — 2, 3, 4, 6, 8, 9, 12

Today I scored ☐ out of 12.

Week 2 — Day 5

Write in the missing numbers and operations.

[1342] —(+ 126)— [1468]

1) [112] —(+ 315)— [ ] —(− 117)— [ ]

2) [ ] —(− 118)— [1420] —(+ 215)— [ ]

3) [4115] —( )— [5230] —( )— [3227]

4) [5705] —(+ 163)— [ ] —(− 240)— [ ]

5) [7005] —( )— [9912] —( )— [4331]

6) [652] —(+ 442)— [ ] —(− 184)— [ ]

7) [ ] —(− 511)— [7668] —( )— [8679]

8) [ ] —(− 530)— [ ] —(+ 343)— [8486]

Today I scored [ ] out of 8.

Week 3 — Day 1

Convert the measurement to the unit given.   3 cm = [30] mm

1) 1 kg = [ ] g

2) 100 cm = [ ] m

3) 10 mm = [ ] cm

4) 2000 m = [ ] km

5) 5 l = [ ] ml

6) 3 km = [ ] m

7) 6 m = [ ] cm

8) 95 mm = [ ] cm

9) 3.2 kg = [ ] g

10) 8930 ml = [ ] l

11) 6.8 l = [ ] ml

12) 6778 g = [ ] kg

Today I scored [ ] out of 12.

Week 3 — Day 2

Solve the calculation. 63 − 13 = 50

1) 47 − 8 =

2) 54 − 23 =

3) 78 − 35 =

4) 83 − 31 =

5) 125 − 16 =

6) 234 − 73 =

7) 683 − 175 =

8) 2.4 − 1.3 =

9) 5.6 − 3.2 =

10) 6.7 − 3.9 =

11) 5.82 − 0.65 =

12) 8.23 − 3.19 =

13) 3.65 − 2.9 =

14) 8.45 − 3.82 =

Today I scored ☐ out of 14.

Week 3 — Day 3

Use the clues to find the number.   It has 2 digits. It is less than 20. Its factors include 7.   14

1) It has 1 digit. Its factors include 2 and 3.

2) It has 2 digits. It is less than 20. Its factors include 3 and 4.

3) It has 2 digits. It is less than 20. Its factors include 3 and 5.

4) It has 2 digits. It is less than 30. Its factors include 2, 4 and 7.

5) It is between 25 and 35. Its factors include 4 and 16.

6) It is between 20 and 30. Its factors include 12.

7) It is between 40 and 60. Its factors include 2 and 11.

8) It is between 40 and 60. Its factors include 9 and 15.

9) It is between 40 and 60. Its factors include 6 and 9.

10) It is between 60 and 80. Its factors include 9 and 12.

Today I scored ☐ out of 10.

Week 3 — Day 4

Fill in the answer.

It was −5 °C. The temperature falls by 2 degrees. What temperature is it now?

−7 °C

1. It was −3 °C. The temperature falls by 3 degrees. What temperature is it now? ☐ °C

2. It was 4 °C. The temperature falls by 5 degrees. What temperature is it now? ☐ °C

3. It was −7 °C. The temperature rises by 4 degrees. What temperature is it now? ☐ °C

4. It was −5 °C. The temperature rises by 9 degrees. What temperature is it now? ☐ °C

5. It was 11 °C. The temperature falls by 15 degrees. What temperature is it now? ☐ °C

6. It was −8 °C. The temperature falls by 5 degrees. What temperature is it now? ☐ °C

7. It was −16 °C. The temperature rises by 12 degrees. What temperature is it now? ☐ °C

8. It was 7 °C. The temperature falls by 20 degrees. What temperature is it now? ☐ °C

9. It was −13 °C. The temperature rises by 19 degrees. What temperature is it now? ☐ °C

10. It was −19 °C. The temperature falls by 7 degrees. What temperature is it now? ☐ °C

Today I scored ☐ out of 10.

Week 3 — Day 5

Work out the new measurement for each alien.

Zig was 2.3 m. He grew 5 cm. How tall is he now? **2.35** m

1) Alog was 4.5 m. She grew 35 cm. How tall is she now? ☐ m

2) Blub was 3.08 m. He grew 40 cm. How tall is he now? ☐ m

3) Col was 2.35 kg. She lost 200 g. How heavy is she now? ☐ kg

4) Dob was 7.85 kg. He gained 30 g. How heavy is he now? ☐ kg

5) Eggle was 4.4 m. She grew 145 cm. How tall is she now? ☐ m

6) Ha was 16.36 kg. He gained 70 g. How heavy is he now? ☐ kg

7) Gur was 5.04 kg. She lost 440 g. How heavy is she now? ☐ kg

8) Flob was 13.19 m. He grew 70 mm. How tall is he now? ☐ m

Today I scored ☐ out of 8.

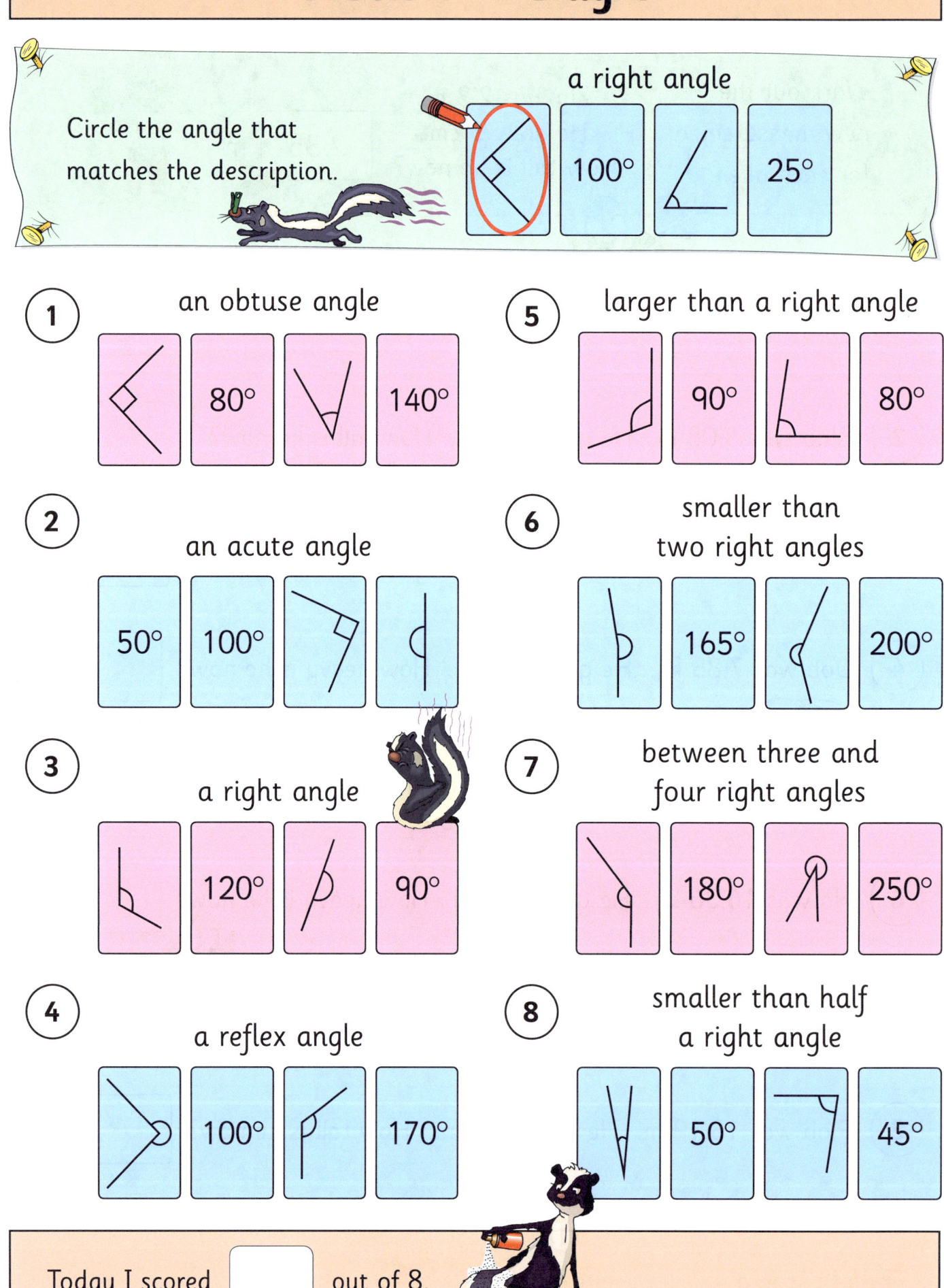

Week 4 — Day 2

Solve the calculation. $\frac{9}{5} + \frac{4}{5} - \frac{3}{5} = \boxed{\frac{10}{5}}$

1) $\frac{2}{8} + \frac{5}{8} + \frac{4}{8} = \boxed{}$

2) $\frac{11}{7} - \frac{4}{7} - \frac{4}{7} = \boxed{}$

3) $\frac{6}{10} - \frac{3}{10} + \frac{12}{10} = \boxed{}$

4) $\frac{18}{9} - \frac{10}{9} - \frac{3}{9} = \boxed{}$

5) $\frac{25}{8} - \frac{15}{8} + \frac{7}{8} = \boxed{}$

6) $\frac{9}{3} + \frac{5}{3} - \frac{6}{3} = \boxed{}$

7) $\frac{14}{12} - \frac{7}{12} + \frac{9}{12} = \boxed{}$

8) $\frac{13}{9} + \frac{12}{9} - \frac{5}{9} = \boxed{}$

9) $\frac{24}{5} - \frac{16}{5} + \frac{9}{5} = \boxed{}$

10) $\frac{6}{3} + \frac{7}{3} - \frac{4}{3} = \boxed{}$

11) $\frac{27}{4} - \frac{19}{4} + \frac{11}{4} = \boxed{}$

12) $\frac{13}{6} - \frac{8}{6} + \frac{7}{6} = \boxed{}$

Today I scored ☐ out of 12.

Week 4 — Day 3

The table shows some approximate conversions between metric and imperial units. Fill in the gaps with the correct sign. Use < or >.

Metric	1 l	1 kg	1 m
Imperial	2 pints	2 pounds	3 feet

3 l > 5 pints

1) 6 l ☐ 10 pints

2) 5 kg ☐ 12 pounds

3) 30 pints ☐ 18 l

4) 18 pints ☐ 8 l

5) 6 pounds ☐ 3.5 kg

6) 8 kg ☐ 15 pounds

7) 14 l ☐ 7 pints

8) 200 m ☐ 670 feet

9) 50 feet ☐ 20 m

10) 12 m ☐ 32 feet

11) 7.5 kg ☐ 18 pounds

12) 25 m ☐ 73 feet

Today I scored ☐ out of 12.

Week 4 — Day 4

Write the correct number of books in the box.

Su has 120 books. $\frac{1}{4}$ of her books are about monsters. How many of her books are about monsters?

30

1) Sona has 360 books. $\frac{1}{6}$ of her books are about fairies. How many of her books are about fairies?

2) Abe has 72 books. $\frac{8}{9}$ of his books are about witches. How many of his books are about witches?

3) Rashid has 270 books. $\frac{2}{3}$ of his books are about aliens. How many of his books are about aliens?

4) Liz has 280 books. $\frac{3}{4}$ of her books are about wizards. How many of her books are about wizards?

5) Rory has 144 books. $\frac{7}{12}$ of his books are about dragons. How many of his books are about dragons?

6) Akua has 180 books. $\frac{5}{6}$ of her books are about spies. How many of her books are about spies?

7) James has 210 books. $\frac{4}{7}$ of his books are about ghosts. How many of his books are about ghosts?

Today I scored ☐ out of 7.

Week 4 — Day 5

The table shows some approximate conversions between metric and imperial units. Complete the sentence about two mice.

Metric	5 cm	100 g	1 m
Imperial	2 inches	4 ounces	3 feet

Max is 6 inches tall and Mali is 20 cm tall. Mali is [5] cm taller than Max.

1 Matilda runs 100 m and Micah runs 250 feet. Matilda runs [ ] feet further than Micah.

2 Mina has 300 g of cheese and Mara has 9 ounces of cheese. Mina has [ ] ounces more cheese than Mara.

3 Milly jumps 8 inches high and Maisy jumps 15 cm high. Milly jumps [ ] inches higher than Maisy.

4 Maria jumps 10 inches high and Milo jumps 30 cm high. Milo jumps [ ] cm higher than Maria.

5 Mona has 75 g of cheese and Molly has 2 ounces of cheese. Mona has [ ] g more cheese than Molly.

6 Missy runs 65 m and Michaela runs 90 feet. Missy runs [ ] m further than Michaela.

Today I scored [ ] out of 6.

Year 5 Mental Maths — Spring Term

Week 5 — Day 1

Fill in the box with a whole number or a mixed number.

1 day = 24 hours

1) 2 weeks = ☐ days

2) 3 hours = ☐ minutes

3) 2 days = ☐ hours

4) 49 days = ☐ weeks

5) 5 hours = ☐ minutes

6) 600 minutes = ☐ hours

7) $\frac{1}{4}$ hour = ☐ minutes

8) $\frac{1}{3}$ hour = ☐ minutes

9) $1\frac{3}{4}$ hours = ☐ minutes

10) 150 minutes = ☐ hours

11) $1\frac{1}{2}$ weeks = ☐ days

12) 72 hours = ☐ days

Today I scored ☐ out of 12.

Week 5 — Day 2

Solve the calculation.   8100 ÷ 9 = 900

1) 40 × 40 =

2) 250 ÷ 5 =

3) 200 × 30 =

4) 1200 ÷ 6 =

5) 500 × 90 =

6) 2100 ÷ 700 =

7) 400 × 80 =

8) 81 000 ÷ 9 =

9) 120 × 120 =

10) 49 000 ÷ 700 =

11) 5000 × 40 =

12) 60 000 ÷ 500 =

Today I scored [ ] out of 12.

Week 5 — Day 3

Work out how many weeks of saving are needed to buy the item.

Alec saves £2 each week. How many weeks will it take him to save up enough for the book?
£7.80 — 4 weeks

1. Manika saves £7 each week. How many weeks will it take her to save up enough for the headphones? £21.00 ☐ weeks

2. Aaron saves £3 each week. How many weeks will it take him to save up enough for the ball? £11.30 ☐ weeks

3. Jade saves £4 each week. How many weeks will it take her to save up enough for the lamp? £23.10 ☐ weeks

4. Callum saves £5 each week. How many weeks will it take him to save up enough for the shoes? £59.70 ☐ weeks

5. Andrea saves £11 each week. How many weeks will it take her to save up enough for the painting? £54.25 ☐ weeks

6. Bryn saves £6 each week. How many weeks will it take him to save up enough for the bicycle? £72.50 ☐ weeks

7. Pippa saves £15 each week. How many weeks will it take her to save up enough for the scooter? £44.00 ☐ weeks

Today I scored ☐ out of 7.

Week 5 — Day 4

Some friends are timing how long it takes for their dogs to find a hidden treat. Fill in the gap with a whole number or a mixed number.

Rover took 2 minutes. This is the same as 120 seconds.

1. Buster took $\frac{3}{4}$ of a minute. This is the same as ☐ seconds.

2. Jessie took 240 seconds. This is the same as ☐ minutes.

3. Alfie took $2\frac{1}{4}$ minutes. This is the same as ☐ seconds.

4. Fido took 75 seconds. This is the same as ☐ minutes.

5. Molly took $\frac{1}{5}$ of a minute. This is the same as ☐ seconds.

6. Bonnie took 150 seconds. This is the same as ☐ minutes.

7. Buddy took $2\frac{1}{3}$ minutes. This is the same as ☐ seconds.

8. Bailey took 72 seconds. This is the same as ☐ minutes.

Today I scored ☐ out of 8.

Week 5 — Day 5

Use the bus timetable to answer the question.
Nia arrives at Rollford bus stop at 17:15. What's the earliest time she can get to Barmton?

18:15

Rollford	Bapworth	Barmton
17:01	17:25	17:43
17:31	17:54	18:15

1 Eli arrives at Rollford bus stop at 18:00. What's the earliest time he can get to Bapworth?

Rollford	Bapworth	Barmton
18:03	18:30	18:49
18:29	19:00	19:18
18:58	19:28	19:48

2 Preeya arrives at Bapworth bus stop at 18:50. What's the earliest time she can get to Barmton?

Bapworth	Barmton	Cobforth
18:30	18:49	19:01
19:00	19:18	19:30
19:28	19:48	20:01

3 Nuala arrives at Cobforth bus stop at 19:00. What's the earliest time she can get to Bunborough?

Barmton	Cobforth	Bunborough
18:49	19:01	19:11
19:18	19:30	19:41
19:48	20:01	20:12

4 Leo arrives at Barmton bus stop at 20:00. What's the earliest time he can get to Bunborough?

Barmton	Cobforth	Bunborough
19:18	19:30	19:41
19:48	20:01	20:12
20:12	20:25	20:37

5 Elmer arrives at Rollford bus stop at 19:10. What's the earliest time he can get to Cobforth?

Rollford	Bapworth	Barmton	Cobforth
18:29	19:00	19:18	19:30
18:58	19:28	19:48	20:01
19:20	19:54	20:12	20:25

6 Fergus arrives at Barmton bus stop at 19:47. What's the earliest time he can get to Bunborough?

Barmton	Cobforth	Bunborough
18:49	19:01	19:11
19:18	19:30	19:41
19:48	20:01	20:12
20:12	20:25	20:37

Today I scored ____ out of 6.

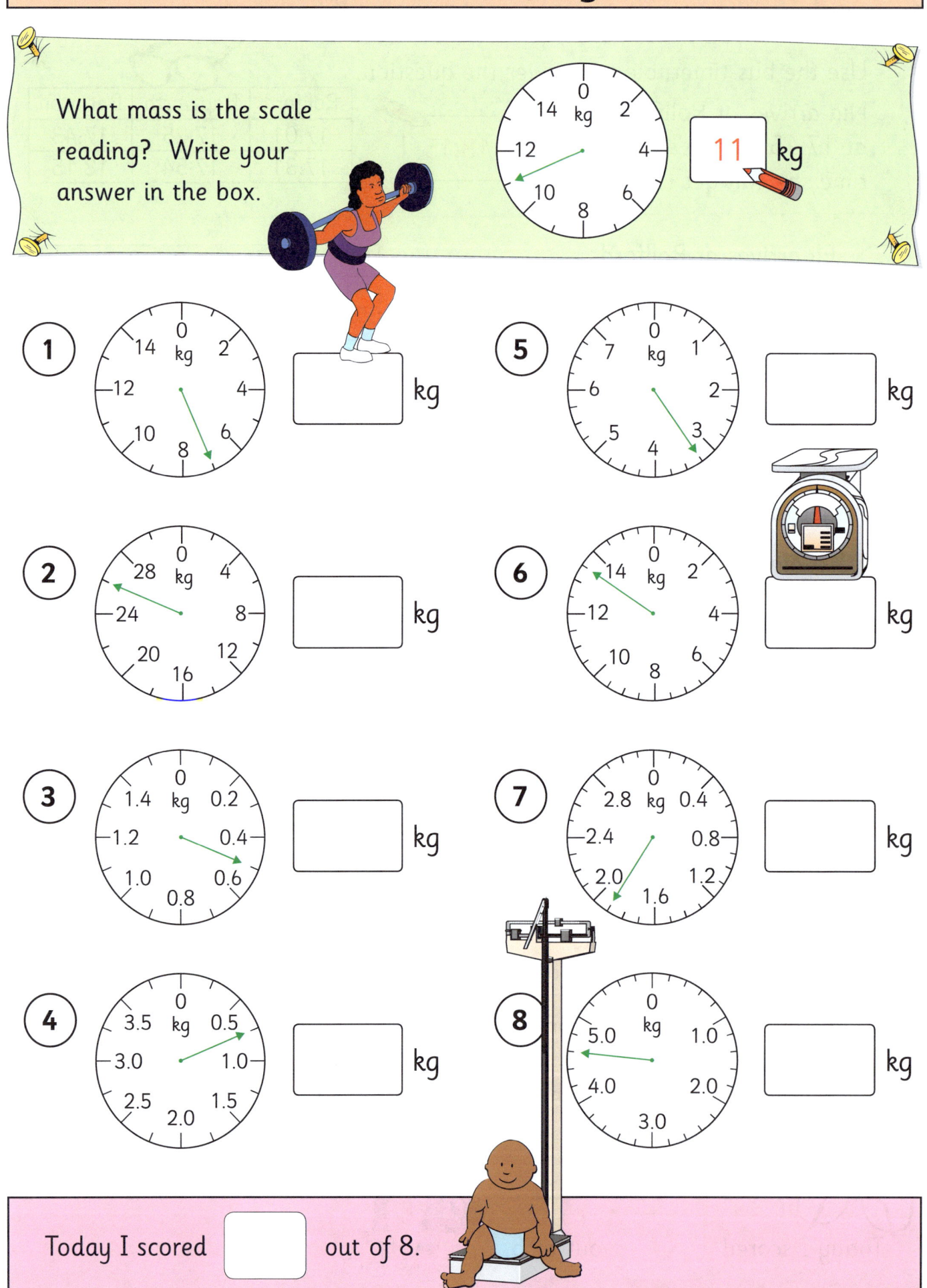

Week 6 — Day 2

Magic beanstalks come in different sizes. Use the information given to work out the answer.

Jack's beanstalk gains 2 kg for every 5 m it grows. How heavy was it when it was 20 m tall?

8 kg

1. Jofra's beanstalk gains 3 kg for every 10 m it grows. How heavy was it when it was 40 m tall? ☐ kg

2. Julie's beanstalk gains 7 kg for every 8 m it grows. How heavy was it when it was 24 m tall? ☐ kg

3. Joe's beanstalk gains 4 kg for every 7 m it grows. How tall was it when it weighed 32 kg? ☐ m

4. Jill's beanstalk gains 7 kg for every 4 m it grows. How heavy was it when it was 36 m tall? ☐ kg

5. Jay's beanstalk gains 6 kg for every 12 m it grows. How tall was it when it weighed 18 kg? ☐ m

6. Jamal's beanstalk gains 8 kg for every 3 m it grows. How tall was it when it weighed 56 kg? ☐ m

7. Jorge's beanstalk gains 9 kg for every 6 m it grows. How tall was it when it weighed 3 kg? ☐ m

8. Jakub's beanstalk gains 3 kg for every 12 m it grows. How heavy was it when it was 2 m tall? ☐ kg

Today I scored ☐ out of 8.

Week 6 — Day 3

Fill in the gaps in the sequence.

$\frac{45}{100}$ → $\frac{47}{100}$ → $\frac{49}{100}$ →

1) $\frac{15}{100}$ → $\frac{17}{100}$ → $\frac{19}{100}$ → ☐ → ☐ →

2) $\frac{27}{80}$ → $\frac{33}{80}$ → $\frac{39}{80}$ → ☐ → ☐ →

3) $\frac{60}{200}$ → ☐ → $\frac{50}{200}$ → $\frac{45}{200}$ → ☐ →

4) $\frac{19}{35}$ → ☐ → ☐ → $\frac{7}{35}$ → $\frac{3}{35}$ →

5) ☐ → $\frac{71}{320}$ → $\frac{80}{320}$ → ☐ → $\frac{98}{320}$ →

6) $\frac{66}{67}$ → ☐ → $\frac{56}{67}$ → ☐ → $\frac{46}{67}$ →

Today I scored ☐ out of 6.

Week 6 — Day 4

What time does the TV show start? Give your answer using the **24 hour clock**.

It's 3:15 am now. The news starts in 1 hour.

It starts at: 04:15

1) It's 7:25 pm now. The cartoon starts in 10 minutes.
It starts at:

2) It's 5:20 am now. The weather starts in 2 hours.
It starts at:

3) It's 2:00 pm now. The soap opera starts in 45 minutes.
It starts at:

4) It's 5:30 pm now. The drama starts in 2 hours 20 minutes.
It starts at:

5) It's 8:35 am now. The science programme starts in 50 minutes.
It starts at:

6) It's 5:15 pm now. The football match starts in 55 minutes.
It starts at:

7) It's 9:20 am now. The reality show starts in 11 hours.
It starts at:

8) It's 2:40 pm now. The film starts in 1 hour 20 minutes.
It starts at:

9) It's 8.55 pm now. The nature programme starts in 40 minutes.
It starts at:

10) It's 11:15 am now. The quiz show starts in 6 hours.
It starts at:

11) It's 11:05 am now. The dance contest starts in 60 minutes.
It starts at:

12) It's 4:10 am now. The cooking show starts in 130 minutes.
It starts at:

Today I scored ☐ out of 12.

Week 6 — Day 5

Calculate the missing volume needed to make the total volume shown on the mug.

milk foam   60 ml
milk   120 ml
coffee   ? ml

60 ml

1)
milk foam   20 ml
milk   ? ml
coffee   40 ml

____ ml

5) milk foam   22 ml
milk   185 ml
coffee   ? ml

____ ml

2)
milk foam   ? ml
milk   180 ml
coffee   50 ml

____ ml

6) milk foam   ? ml
milk   234 ml
coffee   56 ml

____ ml

3)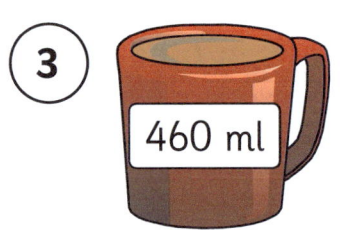
milk foam   35 ml
milk   225 ml
coffee   ? ml

____ ml

7)
milk foam   40 ml
milk   ? ml
coffee   76 ml

____ ml

4)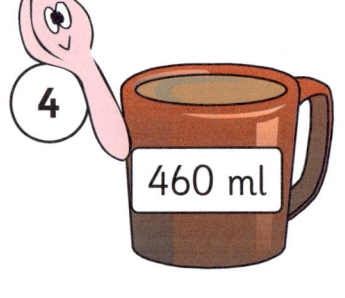
milk foam   55 ml
milk   ? ml
coffee   85 ml

____ ml

8) milk foam   80 ml
milk   360 ml
coffee   ? ml

____ ml

Today I scored ____ out of 8.

Week 7 — Day 1

Circle all the decimals that give the number in the first box when rounded to the nearest whole number.

| 5 | 5.7 | 4.2 | (5.4) | (4.9) | (5.3) | (4.6) | 4.1 |

1) | 5 | 5.7 | 4.2 | 5.4 | 4.9 | 5.3 | 4.6 | 4.1 |

2) | 8 | 8.2 | 7.4 | 7.7 | 8.9 | 8.4 | 7.1 | 8.6 |

3) | 3 | 3.1 | 2.2 | 2.7 | 2.4 | 3.4 | 2.9 | 3.8 |

4) | 14 | 14.3 | 13.7 | 13.4 | 14.9 | 13.6 | 14.4 | 14.6 |

5) | 9 | 8.6 | 9.5 | 9.3 | 8.2 | 8.7 | 9.6 | 8.4 |

6) | 1 | 0.7 | 0.1 | 1.5 | 1.3 | 0.4 | 0.9 | 0.5 |

7) | 6 | 5.5 | 6.3 | 5.4 | 6.5 | 5.1 | 6.6 | 5.7 |

8) | 11 | 11.4 | 10.5 | 10.4 | 10.3 | 11.3 | 11.6 | 10.6 |

Today I scored ☐ out of 8.

Week 7 — Day 2

How many packs are left at the end of the year? Write your answer as a mixed number.

Finn buys some packs of gel pens at the start of the year. There are 10 gel pens in each pack. At the end of the year he has 13 gel pens left.

$1\frac{3}{10}$

1. Farid buys some packs of erasers at the start of the year. There are 3 erasers in each pack. At the end of the year he has 5 erasers left.

2. Aaliyah buys some packs of pens at the start of the year. There are 4 pens in each pack. At the end of the year she has 15 pens left.

3. Kwame buys some packs of crayons at the start of the year. There are 8 crayons in each pack. At the end of the year he has 29 crayons left.

4. Lucia buys some packs of pencils at the start of the year. There are 12 pencils in each pack. At the end of the year she has 25 pencils left.

5. Cal buys some packs of highlighters at the start of the year. There are 6 highlighters in each pack. At the end of the year he has 17 highlighters left.

6. Lee buys some packs of felt tip pens at the start of the year. There are 9 felt tip pens in each pack. At the end of the year he has 38 felt tip pens left.

Today I scored ☐ out of 6.

Week 7 — Day 3

What fraction of the cake has been eaten? Christine ate $\frac{1}{4}$ of the cake and John ate $\frac{3}{8}$ of the cake. $\boxed{\frac{5}{8}}$

1. Ken ate $\frac{3}{10}$ of the cake and Josh ate $\frac{3}{5}$ of the cake.

2. Maja ate $\frac{21}{100}$ of the cake and Ben ate $\frac{7}{10}$ of the cake.

3. Bobby ate $\frac{2}{9}$ of the cake and Joel ate $\frac{2}{3}$ of the cake.

4. Nick ate $\frac{4}{15}$ of the cake and Desi ate $\frac{3}{5}$ of the cake.

5. Rob ate $\frac{7}{18}$ of the cake and Ava ate $\frac{5}{9}$ of the cake.

6. Sam ate $\frac{8}{45}$ of the cake and Alex ate $\frac{4}{9}$ of the cake.

7. Connor ate $\frac{8}{20}$ of the cake and Jin ate $\frac{17}{60}$ of the cake.

8. Lola ate $\frac{11}{42}$ of the cake and Troy ate $\frac{4}{7}$ of the cake.

9. Iga ate $\frac{2}{5}$ of the cake and Grant ate $\frac{53}{100}$ of the cake.

Today I scored ☐ out of 9.

Week 7 — Day 4

Complete the key. ★ + ☾ + ☾ = 1500   Key: ★ = 300, ☾ = 600

1) ★ + ☾ + ☾ = 1300
Key: ★ = ☐, ☾ = 250

2) ★ + ★ + ☾ = 2450
Key: ★ = ☐, ☾ = 1750

3) ★ + ☾ + ☾ + ☾ = 2300
Key: ★ = 500, ☾ = ☐

4) ★ + ★ + ★ + ☾ = 1330
Key: ★ = 310, ☾ = ☐

5) ★ + ☾ + ☾ = 1825
Key: ★ = ☐, ☾ = 705

6) ★ + ★ + ☾ + ☾ = 1520
Key: ★ = 250, ☾ = ☐

7) ★ + ★ + ★ + ☾ = 773
Key: ★ = ☐, ☾ = 410

8) ★ + ☾ + ☾ + ☾ = 4209
Key: ★ = 600, ☾ = ☐

Today I scored ☐ out of 8.

Week 7 — Day 5

Work out the difference between the two fractions. Write your answer as a mixed number if possible.

$\frac{2}{3}$ $\frac{11}{6}$

Difference = $1\frac{1}{6}$

1) $\frac{1}{5}$ $\frac{9}{10}$ Difference =

2) $\frac{13}{14}$ $\frac{2}{7}$ Difference =

3) $\frac{2}{3}$ $\frac{7}{12}$ Difference =

4) $\frac{1}{3}$ $\frac{9}{15}$ Difference =

5) $\frac{1}{4}$ $\frac{17}{8}$ Difference =

6) $\frac{51}{10}$ $\frac{4}{5}$ Difference =

7) $\frac{5}{3}$ $\frac{25}{12}$ Difference =

8) $\frac{2}{3}$ $\frac{33}{6}$ Difference =

Today I scored ☐ out of 8.

Week 8 — Day 1

Write down the total distance travelled by the bus. The bus travels 2.7 km to the first stop, 0.4 km to the second stop and 1.4 km to the last stop. **4.5** km

1. The bus travels 0.3 km to the first stop, 1.1 km to the second stop and 1.4 km to the last stop. ☐ km

2. The bus travels 1.2 km to the first stop, 2.0 km to the second stop and 2.7 km to the last stop. ☐ km

3. The bus travels 3.3 km to the first stop, 0.6 km to the second stop and 2.6 km to the last stop. ☐ km

4. The bus travels 0.7 km to the first stop, 4.5 km to the second stop and 2.7 km to the last stop. ☐ km

5. The bus travels 2.8 km to the first stop, 3.5 km to the second stop and 0.7 km to the last stop. ☐ km

6. The bus travels 0.9 km to the first stop, 1.5 km to the second stop and 1.8 km to the last stop. ☐ km

7. The bus travels 3.6 km to the first stop, 4.8 km to the second stop and 2.7 km to the last stop. ☐ km

Today I scored ☐ out of 7.

Week 8 — Day 2

Write down the number that is being described.

"It's a number between 30 and 40. It's a multiple of 4 and 8."

32

1) "It's a number between 55 and 65. It's a multiple of 7 and 8."

2) "It's a number between 50 and 60. It's a multiple of 6 and 9."

3) "It's a number between 110 and 130. It's a multiple of 5 and 12."

4) "It's a number between 70 and 80. It's a multiple of 3 and 12."

5) "It's a number between 50 and 60. It's a multiple of 4 and 7."

6) "It's a number between 65 and 75. It's a multiple of 4 and 9."

7) "It's a number between 75 and 85. It's a multiple of 3 and 9."

8) "It's a number between 80 and 90. It's a multiple of 3 and 7."

Today I scored ☐ out of 8.

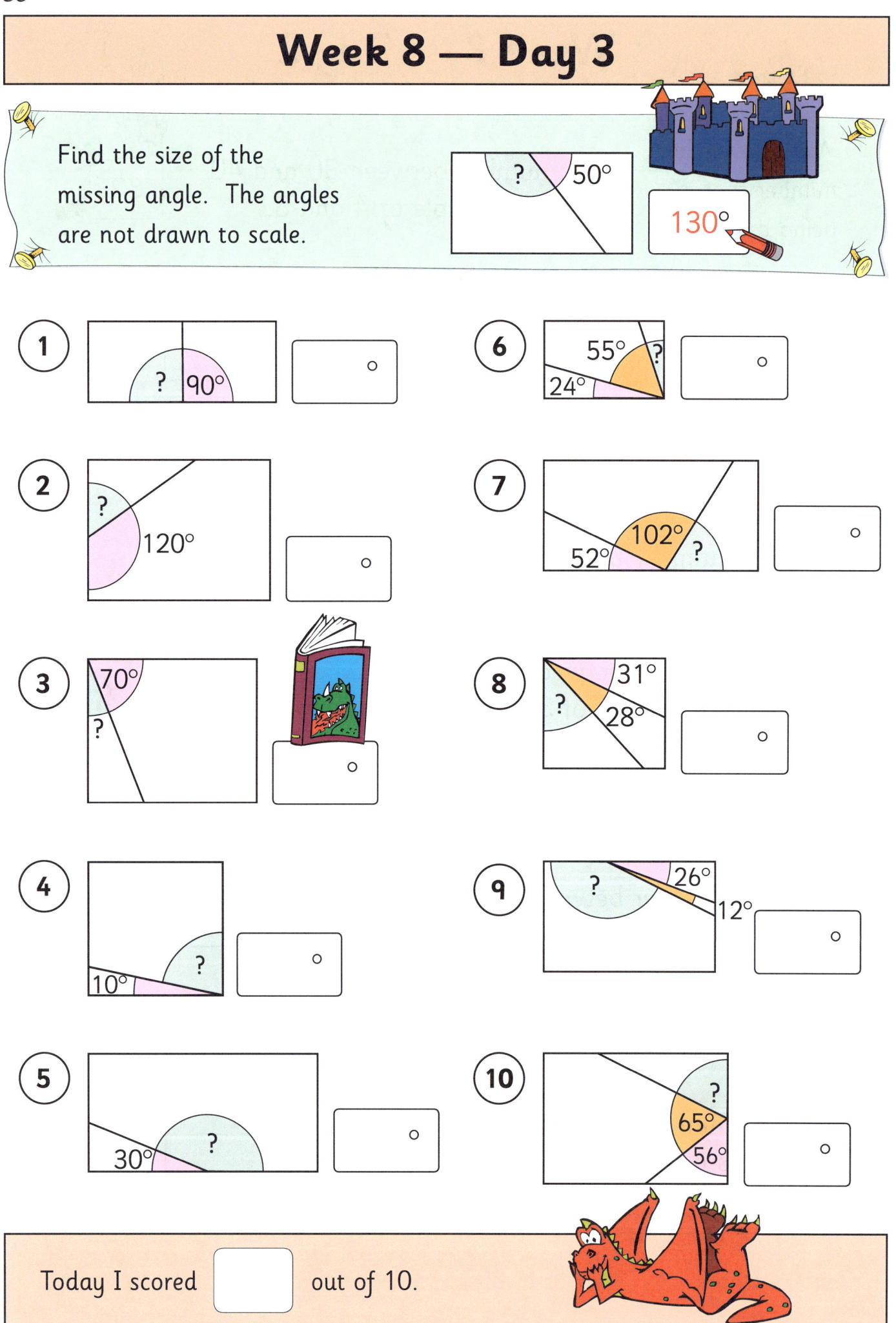

Week 8 — Day 4

The signs show the total number of fans at a match, and the number of fans for each team. What is the missing number?

Total: ?
Hopefield: 18 352
Brombeck: 24 116
→ 42 468

#	Total	Team 1	Team 2	Answer
1	Total: ?	Sadwick: 4948	Rengill: 4051	
2	Total: 53 168	Dufby: 2147	Etterton: ?	
3	Total: 52 342	Cartlam: ?	Farmel: 31 231	
4	Total: ?	Kenforth: 46 335	Gosdal: 12 642	
5	Total: 67 481	Selton: 43 260	Newside: ?	
6	Total: ?	Parside: 21 471	Rampton: 36 295	
7	Total: 46 818	Upver: ?	Torton: 29 406	
8	Total: ?	Ousham: 13 405	Askby: 55 980	
9	Total: ?	Millcroft: 20 267	Longhill: 38 782	
10	Total: 45 738	Yanton: ?	Wigwath: 26 219	

Today I scored ☐ out of 10.

Week 8 — Day 5

What is the answer to the calculation in the number machine?

30 → ×5 → +70 → ÷10 → Round to the nearest 10 → 20

1) 40 → ×6 → +130 → ÷10 → Round to the nearest 10 → ☐

2) 70 → ×3 → +280 → ÷10 → Round to the nearest 10 → ☐

3) 50 → ×8 → −140 → ÷10 → Round to the nearest 10 → ☐

4) 30 → ×9 → +60 → ÷10 → Round to the nearest 10 → ☐

5) 80 → ×7 → −120 → ÷10 → Round to the nearest 10 → ☐

6) 90 → ×8 → −140 → ÷10 → Round to the nearest 10 → ☐

7) 60 → ×12 → +30 → ÷10 → Round to the nearest 10 → ☐

8) 70 → ×11 → −160 → ÷10 → Round to the nearest 10 → ☐

Today I scored ☐ out of 8.

Week 9 — Day 1

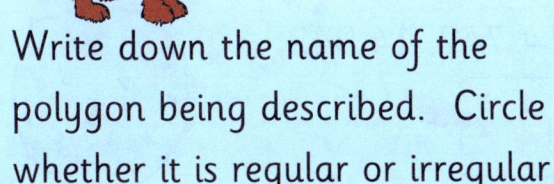

Write down the name of the polygon being described. Circle whether it is regular or irregular.

It has 4 sides. I measure the sides — they are all 4 cm.

(regular) irregular

quadrilateral

1) It has 6 sides. I measure one side — it is 6 cm. I measure another side — it is 3 cm.

regular   irregular

2)  It has 5 sides. I measure the sides — they are all 3.5 cm.

regular   irregular

3) It has 3 sides. I measure one of the angles — it is 90°.

regular   irregular

4) It has 8 sides. I measure the angles — they are all 135°.

regular   irregular

5) It has 10 sides. I measure one side — it is 2 cm. I measure another side — it is 1.5 cm.

regular   irregular

6) It has 7 sides. I measure one of the angles — it is 20°.

regular   irregular

Today I scored [ ] out of 6.

Week 9 — Day 2

Write down the next number in the sequence.

14 542, 14 742, 14 942, ...

15 142

① 4421, 4321, 4221, ...

② 27 243, 25 243, 23 243, ...

③ 13 999, 13 949, 13 899, ...

④ 7643, 7663, 7683, ...

⑤ 63 545, 66 545, 69 545, ...

⑥ 55 877, 53 877, 51 877, ...

⑦ 130 460, 126 460, 122 460, ...

⑧ 3998, 3992, 3986, ...

⑨ 23 551, 34 551, 45 551, ...

⑩ 68 969, 57 969, 46 969, ...

⑪ 2402, 2423, 2444, ...

⑫ 40 786, 40 770, 40 754, ...

Today I scored ☐ out of 12.

Week 9 — Day 3

Find the size of the angle marked P. The diagrams are not drawn to scale.

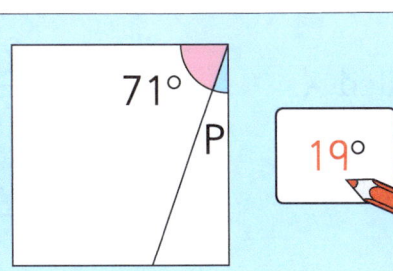 

1)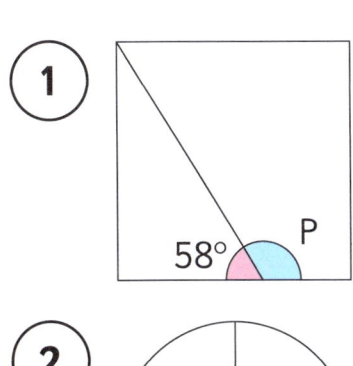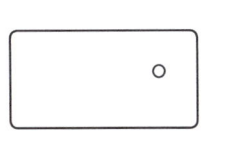

2)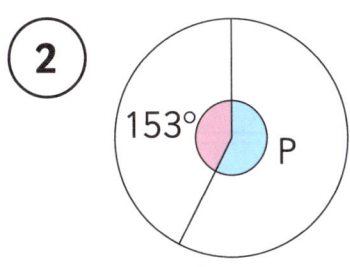

3)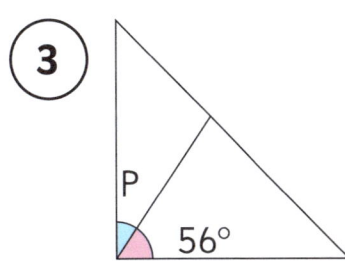

4)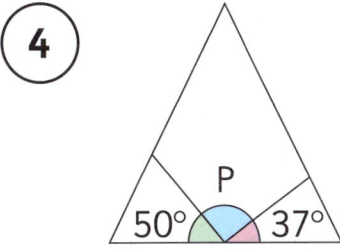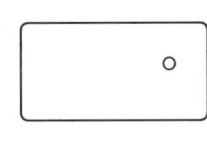

5)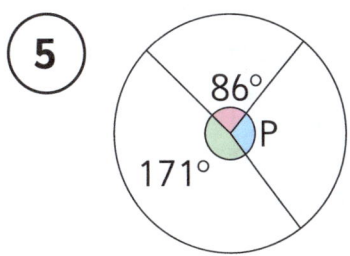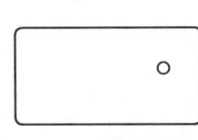

6)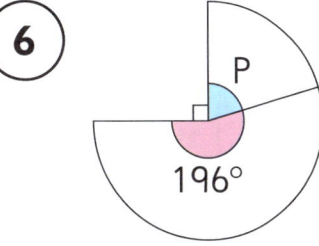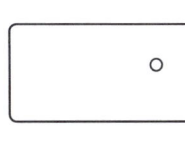

7)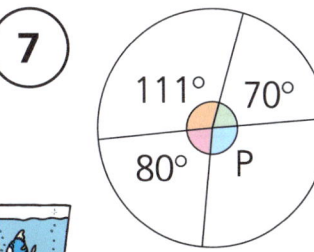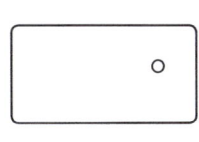

8)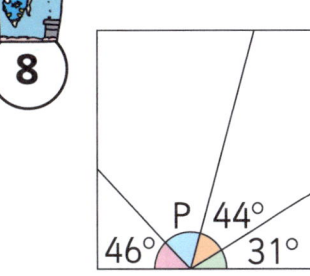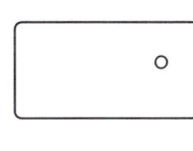

9)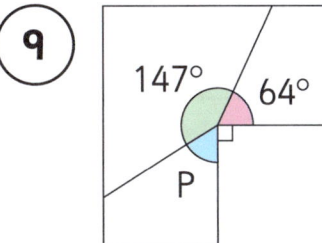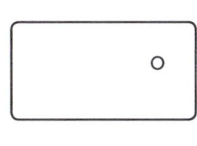

10)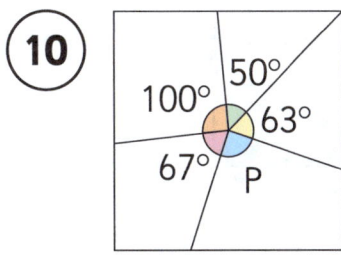

Today I scored  out of 10.

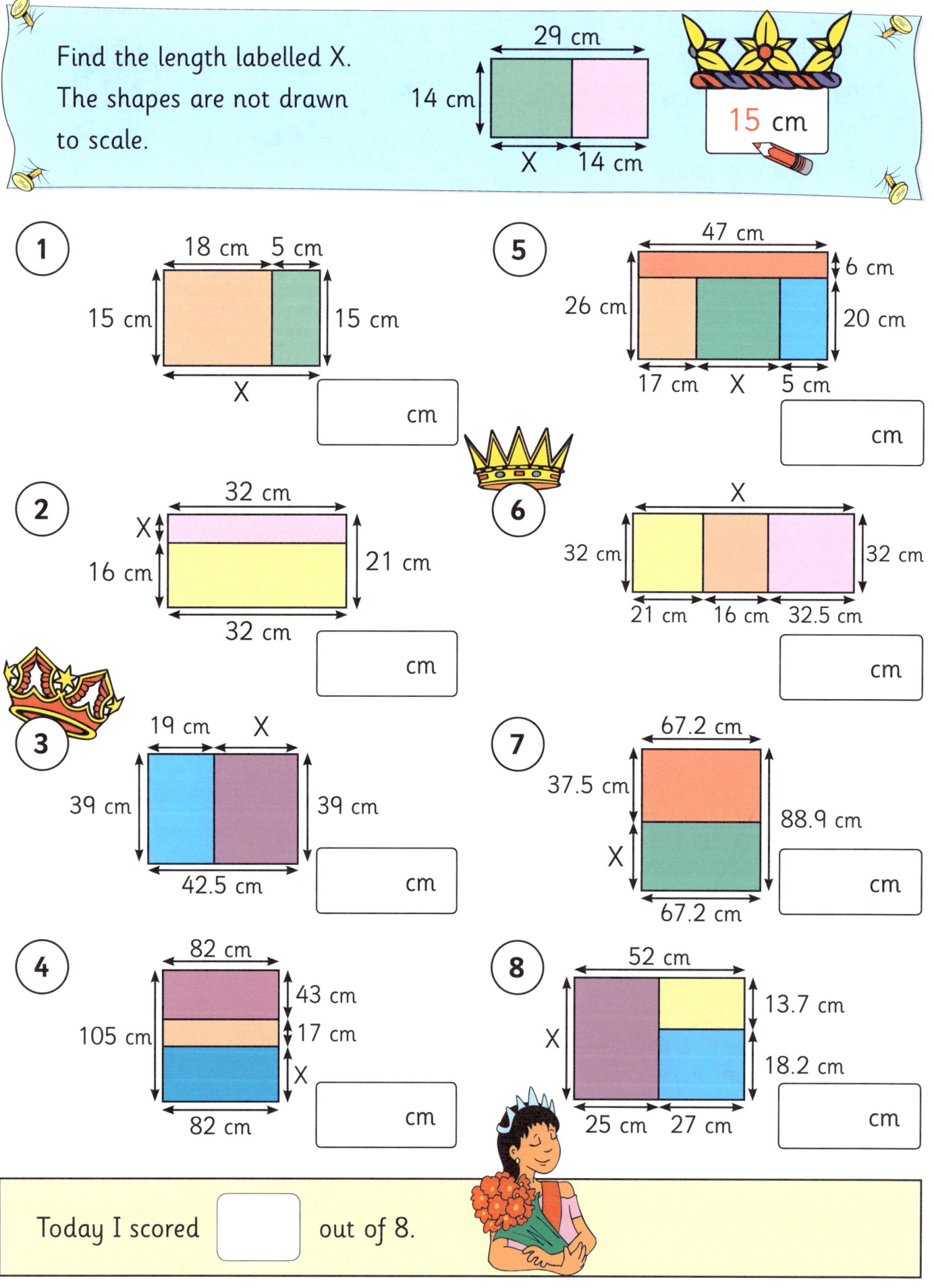

Week 9 — Day 5

Work out how many books will be left over when the bookcases are filled.

The bookcase has 9 shelves. Each shelf holds 50 books. There are 470 books. **20**

1) The bookcase has 10 shelves. Each shelf holds 60 books. There are 625 books.

2) The bookcase has 4 shelves. Each shelf holds 80 books. There are 360 books.

3) The bookcase has 5 shelves. Each shelf holds 50 books. There are 300 books.

4) The bookcase has 11 shelves. Each shelf holds 70 books. There are 800 books.

5) The bookcase has 8 shelves. Each shelf holds 20 books. There are 195 books.

6) The bookcase has 12 shelves. Each shelf holds 50 books. There are 678 books.

7) The bookcase has 7 shelves. Each shelf holds 40 books. There are 320 books.

8) The bookcase has 6 shelves. Each shelf holds 15 books. There are 102 books.

9) The bookcase has 7 shelves. Each shelf holds 800 books. There are 6100 books.

10) The bookcase has 20 shelves. Each shelf holds 25 books. There are 670 books.

Today I scored ____ out of 10.

Week 10 — Day 1

Calculate the perimeter of the rectangle. (The rectangles are not drawn to scale.)

20 cm, 10 cm → **60** cm

1. 5 cm, 4 cm → ___ cm
2. 7 cm, 3 cm → ___ cm
3. 8 cm, 9 cm → ___ cm
4. 5.5 cm, 11 cm → ___ cm
5. 12 cm, 3.5 cm → ___ cm
6. 19.5 cm, 12.5 cm → ___ cm
7. 31 cm, 45 cm → ___ cm
8. 14 cm, 38.5 cm → ___ cm

Today I scored ___ out of 8.

Week 10 — Day 2

A car park has three floors. The signs show the number of spaces in total and the number on each floor. What is the missing number?

Total: 1500 | Floor 1: 550 | Floor 2: 926 | Floor 3: ? → **24**

1. Total: 765 | Floor 1: 245 | Floor 2: 300 | Floor 3: ?

2. Total: 1222 | Floor 1: ? | Floor 2: 11 | Floor 3: 600

3. Total: 2445 | Floor 1: 130 | Floor 2: ? | Floor 3: 1005

4. Total: 5210 | Floor 1: 205 | Floor 2: 3500 | Floor 3: ?

5. Total: 590 | Floor 1: ? | Floor 2: 240 | Floor 3: 12

6. Total: 4232 | Floor 1: 120 | Floor 2: ? | Floor 3: 2500

7. Total: 6318 | Floor 1: ? | Floor 2: 1505 | Floor 3: 3213

8. Total: 5425 | Floor 1: 1112 | Floor 2: ? | Floor 3: 2300

Today I scored ☐ out of 8.

Week 10 — Day 3

Fill in the correct sign. Use <, > or =. $\frac{3}{4}$ > $\frac{5}{8}$

1) $\frac{2}{3}$ ☐ $\frac{3}{6}$

2) $\frac{3}{10}$ ☐ $\frac{1}{5}$

3) $\frac{5}{6}$ ☐ $\frac{11}{12}$

4) $\frac{1}{2}$ ☐ $\frac{3}{8}$

5) $\frac{4}{5}$ ☐ $\frac{12}{15}$

6) $\frac{7}{16}$ ☐ $\frac{5}{8}$

7) $\frac{3}{7}$ ☐ $\frac{10}{21}$

8) $\frac{10}{36}$ ☐ $\frac{7}{18}$

9) $\frac{11}{12}$ ☐ $\frac{31}{36}$

10) $\frac{24}{56}$ ☐ $\frac{3}{7}$

11) $\frac{41}{64}$ ☐ $\frac{21}{32}$

12) $\frac{7}{12}$ ☐ $\frac{61}{72}$

Today I scored ☐ out of 12.

Week 10 — Day 4

Estimate the area of the shape. Each square on the grid is 1 cm². (The grid is not drawn to scale.)

10 cm²

1. ___ cm²

2. ___ cm²

3. ___ cm²

4. ___ cm²

5. ___ cm²

6. ___ cm²

Today I scored ___ out of 6.

Week 10 — Day 5

Calculate the area of the rectangle. (The rectangles are not drawn to scale.)

12 m / 6 m → **72 m²**

1. 50 m × 30 m = ____ m²
2. 40 m × 60 m = ____ m²
3. 90 m × 40 m = ____ m²
4. 120 m × 70 m = ____ m²
5. 15 m × 6 m = ____ m²
6. 4 m × 22.5 m = ____ m²
7. 30.5 m × 30 m = ____ m²
8. 125.8 m × 100 m = ____ m²

Today I scored ____ out of 8.

Week 11 — Day 1

How many tables are needed at the feast?

There are 105 guests and each table seats 5.

21

1. There are 84 guests and each table seats 12.

2. There are 121 guests and each table seats 11.

3. There are 3450 guests and each table seats 10.

4. There are 128 guests and each table seats 4.

5. There are 96 guests and each table seats 8.

6. There are 145 guests and each table seats 5.

7. There are 260 guests and each table seats 20.

8. There are 2000 guests and each table seats 50.

9. There are 5600 guests and each table seats 7.

10. There are 8800 guests and each table seats 8.

11. There are 254 guests and each table seats 8.

12. There are 370 guests and each table seats 25.

Today I scored ☐ out of 12.

Week 11 — Day 2

Circle the image that shows what the shape looks like from above.

1. 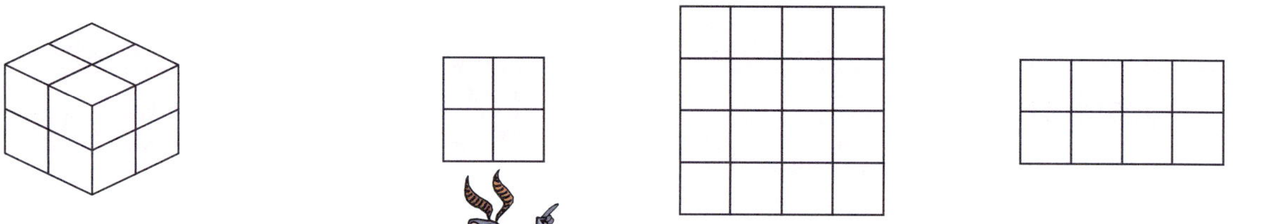
2. 
3. 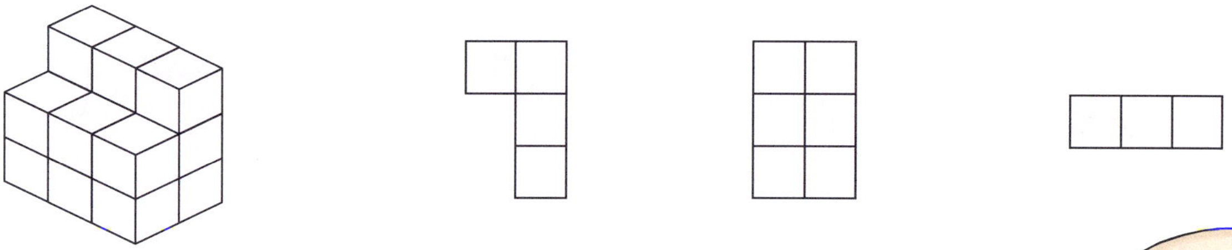
4. 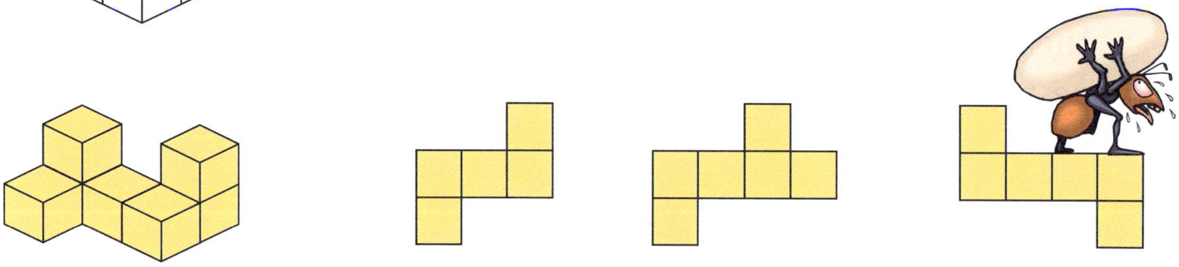
5. 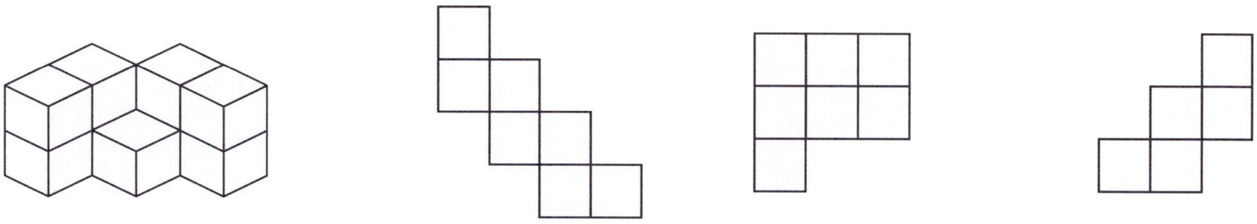
6.

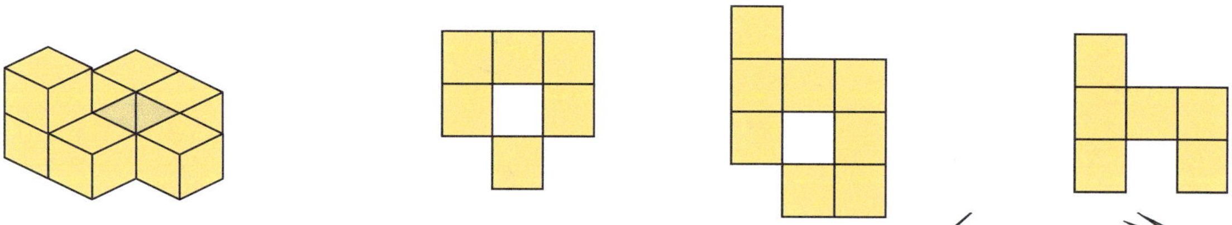

Today I scored  out of 6.

Week 11 — Day 3

Each cube has a volume of 1 cm³. How many **more** cubes are needed to give the shape a volume of 20 cm³?

11

1.

2.

3.

4.

5.

6.

7.

8.

Today I scored ☐ out of 8.

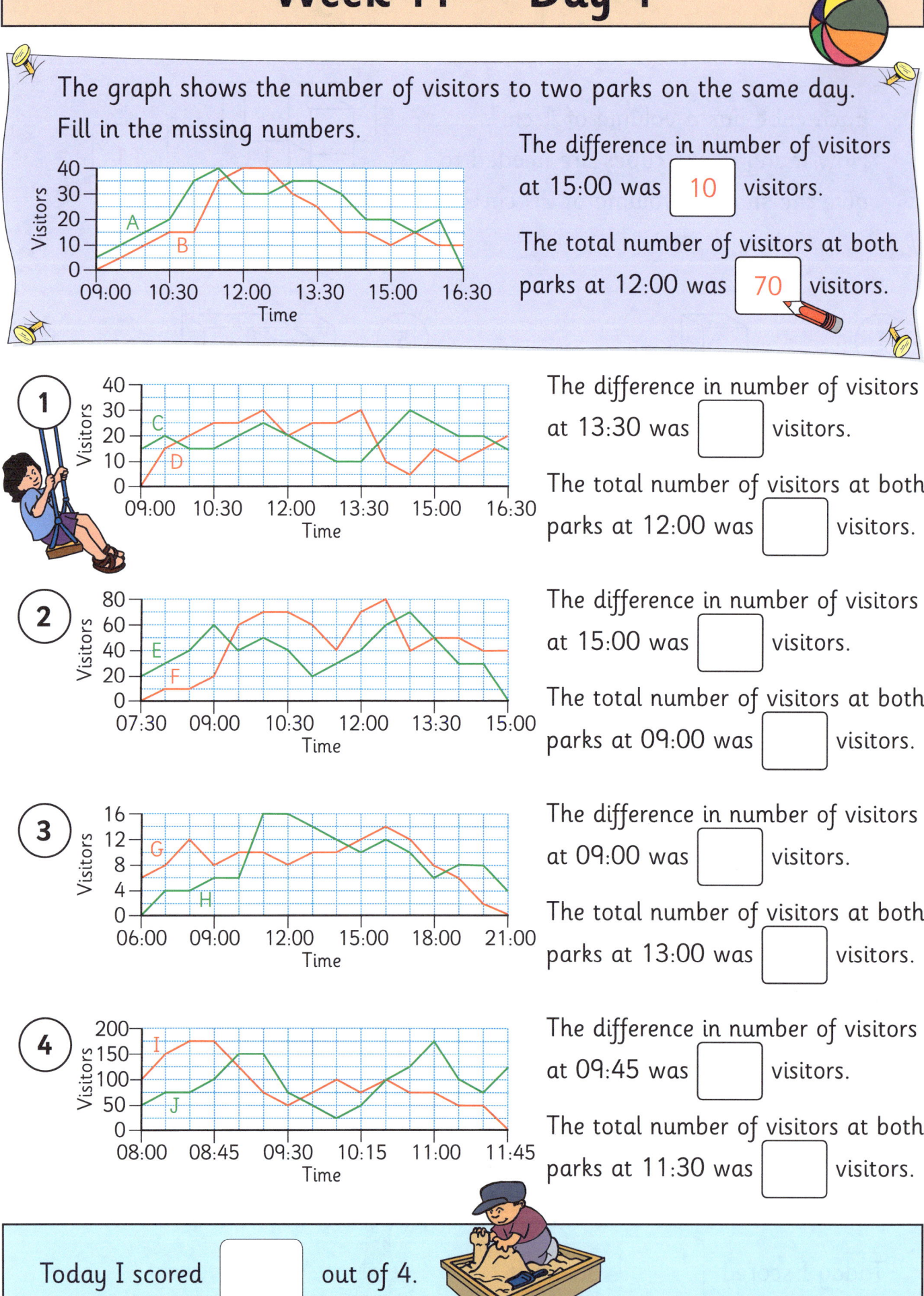

Week 11 — Day 5

Calculate the number of possible combinations, where one option from each group is chosen.

A restaurant has 3 starters, 5 mains and 4 desserts on the menu. How many combinations are there?

60

1. A cinema has 4 types of popcorn and 8 types of fizzy drink. How many combinations are there?

2. A cafe has 2 types of coffee, 6 types of sandwich and 3 types of cake. How many combinations are there?

3. Jonno has 4 hats, 7 scarfs and 2 coats. How many combinations has he got?

4. Ray has 4 pairs of sunglasses, 4 t-shirts and 10 pairs of shorts. How many combinations has he got?

5. A pizza place has 3 sizes of pizza, 8 types of sauce and 3 types of crust. How many combinations are there?

6. Elijah's stickers come in 10 different colours, 3 sizes and 5 shapes. How many combinations are there?

7. A chippy offers 9 mains, 3 sauces and 4 sides. How many combinations are there?

8. Misha's card kit has 3 different sizes, 5 designs and 8 colours. How many combinations are there?

Today I scored ☐ out of 8.

Week 12 — Day 1

Fill in the box to complete the calculation.

425 000 + | 75 000 | = 500 000

1) 12 000 + 56 000 =

2) 32 000 + 14 200 =

3) ☐ − 30 000 = 200 000

4) 33 000 + ☐ = 39 900

5) 27 000 − 8000 =

6) ☐ − 20 000 = 665 000

7) 390 000 − ☐ = 378 000

8) 32 600 + ☐ = 36 920

9) 56 800 + 3120 =

10) ☐ + 310 000 = 790 500

11) 146 500 − 32 300 =

12) 410 000 − ☐ = 278 000

Today I scored ☐ out of 12.

Week 12 — Day 2

Circle all the numbers on the notepad that round to the number in the box.

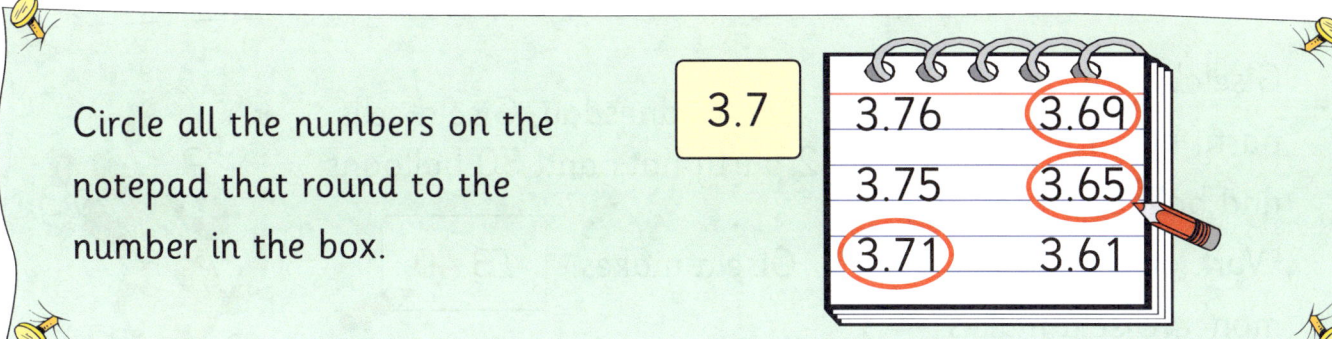

1) **5**
4.39	5.46
4.82	5.09
5.61	4.52

2) **9**
9.21	9.42
8.76	8.99
9.51	8.28

3) **19**
19.81	19.24
19.25	18.37
18.64	18.09

4) **41**
40.55	41.36
40.28	41.08
41.54	40.99

5) **8.6**
8.57	7.66
8.52	8.69
8.61	8.55

6) **9.8**
9.80	9.77
9.79	9.85
9.71	9.83

7) **21.2**
21.09	21.17
21.18	21.28
21.25	21.23

8) **67.9**
67.81	67.85
67.92	67.96
66.83	67.97

Today I scored ☐ out of 8.

Week 12 — Day 3

Gisela's shop sells party hats for 20p and balloons for 10p. Work out how much money Gisela makes.

On Wednesday, Gisela sells 2 party hats and 30 balloons.

Gisela makes: £3.40

1. On Thursday, Gisela sells 3 party hats and 4 balloons.

   Gisela makes: £

2. On Friday, Gisela sells 4 party hats and 5 balloons.

   Gisela makes: £

3. On Saturday, Gisela sells 7 party hats and 6 balloons.

   Gisela makes: £

4. On Sunday, Gisela sells 10 party hats and 7 balloons.

   Gisela makes: £

5. On Monday, Gisela sells 5 party hats and 16 balloons.

   Gisela makes: £

6. On Tuesday, Gisela sells 40 party hats and 11 balloons.

   Gisela makes: £

7. On Wednesday, Gisela sells 23 party hats and 52 balloons.

   Gisela makes: £

8. On Thursday, Gisela sells 15 party hats and 74 balloons.

   Gisela makes: £

Today I scored ☐ out of 8.

Week 12 — Day 4

Complete the calculation. Give your answer as a whole or mixed number.

$4 \times \frac{1}{3} = \boxed{1\frac{1}{3}}$

1) $3 \times \frac{1}{3} =$

2) $5 \times \frac{1}{2} =$

3) $4 \times 2\frac{1}{5} =$

4) $3 \times 1\frac{1}{8} =$

5) $3 \times 2\frac{2}{7} =$

6) $7 \times \frac{1}{4} =$

7) $5 \times 1\frac{1}{3} =$

8) $8 \times \frac{3}{4} =$

9) $2 \times 2\frac{3}{5} =$

10) $5 \times 2\frac{3}{8} =$

11) $5 \times 3\frac{2}{5} =$

12) $10 \times 3\frac{1}{7} =$

Today I scored ☐ out of 12.

Week 12 — Day 5

Follow the instructions on the arrows to round each measurement.

4672.1 g → to the nearest g → 4672 g
4672.1 g → to the nearest kg → 5 kg

1) 376.6 g → to the nearest g → ___ g
   376.6 g → to the nearest kg → ___ kg

2) 55.6 cm → to the nearest cm → ___ cm
   55.6 cm → to the nearest m → ___ m

3) 4588.8 m → to the nearest m → ___ m
   4588.8 m → to the nearest km → ___ km

4) 2138.5 ml → to the nearest ml → ___ ml
   2138.5 ml → to the nearest l → ___ l

5) 2604.14 g → to the nearest g → ___ g
   2604.14 g → to the nearest kg → ___ kg

6) 891.87 cm → to the nearest cm → ___ cm
   891.87 cm → to the nearest m → ___ m

7) 7190.85 m → to the nearest m → ___ m
   7190.85 m → to the nearest km → ___ km

8) 8799.59 ml → to the nearest ml → ___ ml
   8799.59 ml → to the nearest l → ___ l

Today I scored ___ out of 8.

Answers

Week 1 — Day 1

1. $\frac{3}{10}$
2. $\frac{7}{10}$
3. $\frac{1}{2}$
4. $\frac{39}{100}$
5. $\frac{83}{100}$
6. $\frac{91}{100}$
7. $\frac{1}{4}$
8. $\frac{3}{4}$
9. $\frac{1}{5}$
10. $\frac{4}{5}$
11. $\frac{8}{20}$
12. $\frac{18}{20}$

Week 1 — Day 2

1. Wednesday and Thursday, 5
2. Tuesday and Wednesday, 5
3. Tuesday and Wednesday, 4
4. Wednesday and Thursday, 4
5. Thursday and Friday, 9
6. Wednesday and Thursday, 13

Week 1 — Day 3

1. −1
2. 4
3. −9
4. 10
5. 3
6. 15
7. −5
8. −3
9. 6
10. 3
11. 5
12. −7

Week 1 — Day 4

1. + 10, 82 344, 82 364
2. + 200, 56 901, 57 301
3. − 30, 6833, 6773
4. + 2000, 4529, 8529
5. − 5000, 33 318, 23 318
6. − 15 000, 40 078, 10 078

Week 1 — Day 5

1. 5
2. 6
3. 8
4. 10
5. 12
6. 10
7. 20
8. 15
9. 20
10. 10
11. 8
12. 12

Week 2 — Day 1

1. 8510
2. 2.5
3. 324
4. 75.53
5. 441.2
6. 3.5
7. 1200
8. 0.07
9. 5566
10. 6.08
11. 330
12. 1.85

Week 2 — Day 2

1. £26.50
2. £31.10
3. £18.75
4. £28.50
5. £48.20
6. £19.85
7. £31.35
8. £12.80

Week 2 — Day 3

1. 1.7 m
2. 420 g
3. 2.7 m
4. 350 ml
5. 10 cm
6. 400 g
7. 40 cm
8. 570 ml
9. 15.3 m
10. 13 m
11. 30 g
12. 400 ml

Week 2 — Day 4

1. 1, 2
2. 2, 4, 8
3. 1, 5
4. 11
5. 7
6. 2, 4
7. 1, 5, 10
8. 9
9. 3, 5, 15
10. 2, 8
11. 1, 3, 9
12. 2, 3, 4, 6, 8, 12

Week 2 — Day 5

1. 427, 310
2. 1538, 1635
3. + 1115, − 2003
4. 5868, 5628
5. + 2907, − 5581
6. 1094, 910
7. 8179, + 1011
8. 8673, 8143

Week 3 — Day 1

1. 1000 g
2. 1 m
3. 1 cm
4. 2 km
5. 5000 ml
6. 3000 m
7. 600 cm
8. 9.5 cm
9. 3200 g
10. 8.93 l
11. 6800 ml
12. 6.778 kg

Week 3 — Day 2

1. 39
2. 31
3. 43
4. 52
5. 109
6. 161
7. 508
8. 1.1
9. 2.4
10. 2.8
11. 5.17
12. 5.04
13. 0.75
14. 4.63

Week 3 — Day 3

1. 6
2. 12
3. 15
4. 28
5. 32
6. 24
7. 44
8. 45
9. 54
10. 72

Week 3 — Day 4

1. −6 °C
2. −1 °C
3. −3 °C
4. 4 °C
5. −4 °C
6. −13 °C
7. −4 °C
8. −13 °C
9. 6 °C
10. −26 °C

Week 3 — Day 5

1. 4.85 m
2. 3.48 m
3. 2.15 kg
4. 7.88 kg
5. 5.85 m
6. 16.43 kg
7. 4.6 kg
8. 13.26 m

Week 4 — Day 1
1. 140°
2. 50°
3. 90°
4.
5.
6. 165°
7.
8.

Week 4 — Day 2
1. $\frac{11}{8}$
2. $\frac{3}{7}$
3. $\frac{15}{10}$ or $\frac{3}{2}$
4. $\frac{5}{9}$
5. $\frac{17}{8}$
6. $\frac{8}{3}$
7. $\frac{16}{12}$ or $\frac{4}{3}$
8. $\frac{20}{9}$
9. $\frac{17}{5}$
10. $\frac{9}{3}$ or $\frac{3}{1}$
11. $\frac{19}{4}$
12. $\frac{12}{6}$ or $\frac{2}{1}$

Week 4 — Day 3
1. >
2. <
3. <
4. >
5. <
6. >
7. >
8. <
9. <
10. >
11. <
12. >

Week 4 — Day 4
1. 60
2. 64
3. 180
4. 210
5. 84
6. 150
7. 120

Week 4 — Day 5
1. 50 feet
2. 3 ounces
3. 2 inches
4. 5 cm
5. 25 g
6. 35 m

Week 5 — Day 1
1. 14 days
2. 180 minutes
3. 48 hours
4. 7 weeks
5. 300 minutes
6. 10 hours
7. 15 minutes
8. 20 minutes
9. 105 minutes
10. $2\frac{1}{2}$ hours
11. $10\frac{1}{2}$ days
12. 3 days

Week 5 — Day 2
1. 1600
2. 50
3. 6000
4. 200
5. 45 000
6. 3
7. 32 000
8. 9000
9. 14 400
10. 70
11. 200 000
12. 120

Week 5 — Day 3
1. 3 weeks
2. 4 weeks
3. 6 weeks
4. 12 weeks
5. 5 weeks
6. 13 weeks
7. 3 weeks

Week 5 — Day 4
1. 45 seconds
2. 4 minutes
3. 135 seconds
4. $1\frac{1}{4}$ minutes
5. 12 seconds
6. $2\frac{1}{2}$ minutes
7. 140 seconds
8. $1\frac{1}{5}$ minutes

Week 5 — Day 5
1. 18:30
2. 19:18
3. 19:11
4. 20:37
5. 20:25
6. 20:12

Week 6 — Day 1
1. 7 kg
2. 26 kg
3. 0.5 kg
4. 0.75 kg
5. 3.25 kg
6. 13.5 kg
7. 1.9 kg
8. 4.6 kg

Week 6 — Day 2
1. 12 kg
2. 21 kg
3. 56 m
4. 63 kg
5. 36 m
6. 21 m
7. 2 m
8. 0.5 kg

Week 6 — Day 3
1. $\frac{15}{100}, \frac{17}{100}, \frac{19}{100}, \mathbf{\frac{21}{100}}, \mathbf{\frac{23}{100}}$
2. $\frac{27}{80}, \frac{33}{80}, \frac{39}{80}, \mathbf{\frac{45}{80}}, \mathbf{\frac{51}{80}}$
3. $\frac{60}{200}, \mathbf{\frac{55}{200}}, \frac{50}{200}, \frac{45}{200}, \mathbf{\frac{40}{200}}$
4. $\frac{19}{35}, \mathbf{\frac{15}{35}}, \mathbf{\frac{11}{35}}, \frac{7}{35}, \frac{3}{35}$
5. $\mathbf{\frac{62}{320}}, \frac{71}{320}, \frac{80}{320}, \mathbf{\frac{89}{320}}, \frac{98}{320}$
6. $\frac{66}{67}, \mathbf{\frac{61}{67}}, \frac{56}{67}, \mathbf{\frac{51}{67}}, \frac{46}{67}$

Week 6 — Day 4
1. 19:35
2. 07:20
3. 14:45
4. 19:50
5. 09:25
6. 18:10
7. 20:20
8. 16:00
9. 21:35
10. 17:15
11. 12:05
12. 06:20

Week 6 — Day 5
1. 180 ml
2. 10 ml
3. 200 ml
4. 320 ml
5. 18 ml
6. 46 ml
7. 84 ml
8. 130 ml

Week 7 — Day 1
1. 5.4, 4.9, 5.3, 4.6
2. 8.2, 7.7, 8.4
3. 3.1, 2.7, 3.4, 2.9
4. 14.3, 13.7, 13.6, 14.4
5. 8.6, 9.3, 8.7
6. 0.7, 1.3, 0.9, 0.5
7. 5.5, 6.3, 5.7
8. 11.4, 10.5, 11.3, 10.6

Week 7 — Day 2
1. $1\frac{2}{3}$
2. $3\frac{3}{4}$
3. $3\frac{5}{8}$
4. $2\frac{1}{12}$
5. $2\frac{5}{6}$
6. $4\frac{2}{9}$

Week 7 — Day 3
1. $\frac{9}{10}$
2. $\frac{91}{100}$
3. $\frac{8}{9}$
4. $\frac{13}{15}$
5. $\frac{17}{18}$
6. $\frac{28}{45}$
7. $\frac{41}{60}$
8. $\frac{35}{42}$
9. $\frac{93}{100}$

Week 7 — Day 4
1. 800
2. 350
3. 600
4. 400
5. 415
6. 510
7. 121
8. 1203

Week 7 — Day 5
1. $\frac{7}{10}$
2. $\frac{9}{14}$
3. $\frac{1}{12}$
4. $\frac{4}{15}$
5. $1\frac{7}{8}$
6. $4\frac{3}{10}$
7. $\frac{5}{12}$
8. $4\frac{5}{6}$

Week 8 — Day 1
1. 2.8 km
2. 5.9 km
3. 6.5 km
4. 7.9 km
5. 7 km
6. 4.2 km
7. 11.1 km

Week 8 — Day 2
1. 56
2. 54
3. 120
4. 72
5. 56
6. 72
7. 81
8. 84

Week 8 — Day 3
1. 90°
2. 60°
3. 20°
4. 80°
5. 150°
6. 11°
7. 26°
8. 31°
9. 142°
10. 59°

Week 8 — Day 4
1. 8999
2. 51 021
3. 21 111
4. 58 977
5. 24 221
6. 57 766
7. 17 412
8. 69 385
9. 59 049
10. 19 519

Week 8 — Day 5
1. 40
2. 50
3. 30
4. 30
5. 40
6. 60
7. 80
8. 60

Week 9 — Day 1
1. irregular hexagon
2. regular pentagon
3. irregular triangle (or right angled triangle)
4. regular octagon
5. irregular decagon
6. irregular heptagon

Week 9 — Day 2
1. 4121
2. 21 243
3. 13 849
4. 7703
5. 72 545
6. 49 877
7. 118 460
8. 3980
9. 56 551
10. 35 969
11. 2465
12. 40 738

Week 9 — Day 3
1. 122°
2. 207°
3. 34°
4. 93°
5. 103°
6. 74°
7. 99°
8. 59°
9. 59°
10. 80°

Week 9 — Day 4
1. 23 cm
2. 5 cm
3. 23.5 cm
4. 45 cm
5. 25 cm
6. 69.5 cm
7. 51.4 cm
8. 31.9 cm

Week 9 — Day 5
1. 25
2. 40
3. 50
4. 30
5. 35
6. 78
7. 40
8. 12
9. 500
10. 170

Week 10 — Day 1
1. 18 cm
2. 20 cm
3. 34 cm
4. 33 cm
5. 31 cm
6. 64 cm
7. 152 cm
8. 105 cm

Week 10 — Day 2
1. 220
2. 611
3. 1310
4. 1505
5. 338
6. 1612
7. 1600
8. 2013

Week 10 — Day 3
1. >
2. >
3. <
4. >
5. =
6. <
7. <
8. <
9. >
10. =
11. <
12. <

Week 10 — Day 4
1. 14 cm²
2. 14.5 cm²
3. 16.5 cm²
4. 11.5 cm²
5. Accept between 11.5 and 12.5 cm².
6. Accept between 16 and 18 cm².

Week 10 — Day 5
1. 1500 m²
2. 2400 m²
3. 3600 m²
4. 8400 m²
5. 90 m²
6. 90 m²
7. 915 m²
8. 12 580 m²

Week 11 — Day 1
1. 7
2. 11
3. 345
4. 32
5. 12
6. 29
7. 13
8. 40
9. 800
10. 1100
11. 32
12. 15

Week 11 — Day 2
1. [2×2 grid, unshaded]
2. [1×3 column, shaded]
3. [3×3 grid, unshaded]
4. [L-shape, shaded]
5. [shape, unshaded]
6. [shape, shaded]

Week 11 — Day 3
1. 14
2. 11
3. 12
4. 10
5. 9
6. 9
7. 7
8. 8

Week 11 — Day 4
1. 20, 40
2. 40, 80
3. 2, 24
4. 25, 125

Week 11 — Day 5
1. 32
2. 36
3. 56
4. 160
5. 72
6. 150
7. 108
8. 120

Week 12 — Day 1
1. 68 000
2. 46 200
3. 230 000
4. 6900
5. 19 000
6. 685 000
7. 12 000
8. 4320
9. 59 920
10. 480 500
11. 114 200
12. 132 000

Week 12 — Day 2
1. 4.82, 5.46, 5.09, 4.52
2. 9.21, 8.76, 9.42, 8.99
3. 19.25, 18.64, 19.24
4. 40.55, 41.36, 41.08, 40.99
5. 8.57, 8.61, 8.55
6. 9.80, 9.79, 9.77, 9.83
7. 21.18, 21.17, 21.23
8. 67.92, 67.85

Week 12 — Day 3
1. £1.00
2. £1.30
3. £2.00
4. £2.70
5. £2.60
6. £9.10
7. £9.80
8. £10.40

Week 12 — Day 4
1. 1
2. $2\frac{1}{2}$
3. $8\frac{4}{5}$
4. $3\frac{3}{8}$
5. $6\frac{6}{7}$
6. $1\frac{3}{4}$
7. $6\frac{2}{3}$
8. 6
9. $5\frac{1}{5}$
10. $11\frac{7}{8}$
11. 17
12. $31\frac{3}{7}$

Week 12 — Day 5
1. 377 g, 0 kg
2. 56 cm, 1 m
3. 4589 m, 5 km
4. 2139 ml, 2 l
5. 2604 g, 3 kg
6. 892 cm, 9 m
7. 7191 m, 7 km
8. 8800 ml, 9 l